YOUR KNOWLEDGE HAS VALUE

- We will publish your bachelor's and master's thesis, essays and papers

- Your own eBook and book - sold worldwide in all relevant shops

- Earn money with each sale

Upload your text at www.GRIN.com
and publish for free

Bibliographic information published by the German National Library:

The German National Library lists this publication in the National Bibliography; detailed bibliographic data are available on the Internet at http://dnb.dnb.de .

This book is copyright material and must not be copied, reproduced, transferred, distributed, leased, licensed or publicly performed or used in any way except as specifically permitted in writing by the publishers, as allowed under the terms and conditions under which it was purchased or as strictly permitted by applicable copyright law. Any unauthorized distribution or use of this text may be a direct infringement of the author s and publisher s rights and those responsible may be liable in law accordingly.

Imprint:

Copyright © 2017 GRIN Verlag
Print and binding: Books on Demand GmbH, Norderstedt Germany
ISBN: 9783668694996

This book at GRIN:

https://www.grin.com/document/424170

Anonym

Sexism in Tommy Wiseau's film "The Room" and its YouTube reviews

GRIN Verlag

GRIN - Your knowledge has value

Since its foundation in 1998, GRIN has specialized in publishing academic texts by students, college teachers and other academics as e-book and printed book. The website www.grin.com is an ideal platform for presenting term papers, final papers, scientific essays, dissertations and specialist books.

Visit us on the internet:

http://www.grin.com/

http://www.facebook.com/grincom

http://www.twitter.com/grin_com

Sexism in *the Room* and its YouTube reviews

SS 2017

Department of English and American Studies

University of Vienna

Sexism in *The Room* and its YouTube reviews

ABSTRACT

In this paper I would like to discuss the role of gender in the reception of Tommy Wiseau's film *The Room*. In particular I will analyse how four YouTube review channels react to how the female main character Lisa is treated by the film. The focus of my research will be the comic value these reviewers find in Lisa's actions with the goal of revealing some of their sexist or misogynistic assumptions about gender by what they find humorous. In order to do this, firstly I will discuss and describe the main scenes I will look at more closely and explain why they seem problematic from a gender, humour and film studies perspective. The first scene this paper focuses on shows a conversation where Lisa tells her mother that Johnny hit her. In the second scene, a story of a woman that has been beaten is recounted and, finally, in the last scene Lisa is made responsible for Johnny's death. Secondly, I will introduce my chosen YouTube channels: CinemaSins, Channel Awesome, I Hate Everything and FanboyFlicks and then observe how they perceive the chosen scenes and whether they ignore the scenes and Lisa's treatment or not. Additionally, I will compare these channels by looking at how they view and describe Lisa in general. As a last step I demonstrate that some of the reviewers I chose ignore the scenes and Lisa's treatment in general. Based on my discoveries, I assume to find sexist standards in the majority of the channels, especially when they ignore or find humour in scenes in which Lisa is mistreated.

THE PROBLEMATICS OF THE SCENES

This section will describe the scenes and put them in context with the theory of film in order to show how the film is inherently sexist. Summed up, it is about Johnny, a banker whose fiancée Lisa does not love him anymore and has an affair with his best friend Mark. After various subplots that are not actually explained, Mark and Johnny get into a fight at the latter's birthday party and Johnny proves that Lisa is cheating on him. He then kills himself and the film ends. The three scenes I chose as a base for my research have one thing in common: they show the sexist standards of various protagonists, which can be seen in how they treat and talk about women. This disempowerment is common in films, as Laura Mulvey writes in her essay:

[w]oman, then, stands in patriarchal culture as signifier for the male other, bound by a symbolic order in which man can live out his fantasies and obsessions through linguistic command, by imposing them on the silent image of woman still tied to her place as bearer of meaning, not maker of meaning. (Mulvey 484)

This means that the female figure should be silent and passive, she is "woman as spectacle" (Mulvey 488). With the example of pornographic movies, melodramas and horror movies, Williams described women in film as "embodiments of pleasure, fear, and pain" (Williams 210). Lisa is exactly that, the archetype of the bad female character; an archetype being a popular and often occurring trope (Eco 464). Together with that, woman in general "symbolizes the castration threat", as Mulvey (483) states and the men have to fight against that. They do so by, for instance, saving or punishing her (Mulvey 489). Lisa is not exactly passive, she does seem to drive the story and, additionally, she embodies the bad. Therefore, she has to be punished by man, which can be seen in the following scenes:

The first scene shows Lisa talking to her mother Claudette, telling her that she does not love Johnny anymore and wants to leave him. Her mother, however, advises against that as she does not believe that Lisa can support herself. While this is already quite sexist, my focus lies on what happens next: Lisa reveals to her mother that Johnny has hit her while drunk, to which Claudette's only answer is: "But Johnny doesn't drink" (The Room 28:30-28:32). Despite the fact that the story is a lie, her mother's basically non-existent reaction is problematic. Claudette's views are patriarchal, demonstrated by her advice that Lisa should not leave Johnny. The film, in the form of Lisa's mother, implies that there is nothing wrong with Johnny hitting Lisa. Indeed, it can be seen as a punishment and, as Mulvey's quote at the beginning of this section suggests, the woman, Lisa, should take what the men do to her silently. The second scene I chose is part of the so-called 'rooftop-scene' in which Johnny and Mark have a deep conversation. This paper is going to focus on a story Mark tells Johnny about a girl he knew who was beaten up badly by one of her lovers. Johnny's response to this story is laughter and the exclamation: "What a story, Mark!" (The Room 38:34-38:38), which also seems inappropriate. This reaction can be seen as sexist for another reason: as Martin writes, humorous attitudes towards certain behaviours like, in this case, a man beating up a woman, "can communicate implicit expectations and rules concerning the kinds of behavior that are considered acceptable" (Martin, *The Psychology of Humor* 119). As well as that, it can, again, be seen as a punishment for women being active and symbolising a threat in the eyes of men. The last scene is one of the final moments of the film, where Lisa and Mark are crying over Johnny's corpse. In this scene Mark tells Lisa that she alone is responsible for Johnny's death

(The Room 1:34:33-1:34:57). Of course, this may be because he is grief-stricken, but still, he blames their affair on her and it is not the first time for him to do so: In an earlier scene, he blames her for the sex they just had (The Room 19:26-19:24). In traditional films, as already mentioned, the female, in contrast to the male, part should not be active and thus only Lisa should be burdened with Johnny's death because she steps out of her boundaries. One last time she signifies the ultimate bad and is, in this case, punished for seducing Mark and taking his power away.

REACTIONS OF THE REVIEWERS

In this part this paper focuses on how four different YouTube channels perceive these scenes, and, by putting them in contrast with humour and gender theory, how their reactions show inherent sexist values. In order to this I chose CinemaSins, Channel Awesome, I Hate Everything, henceforth IHE, and FanboyFlicks. This is because these are a few of the biggest channels that focus on reviewing films. Of course these are only some of many reviews on *The Room* and because of that, this paper does not claim to have all the information needed for a general conclusion. Because they identify the film as so bad that it is actually funny, we may conclude that what they leave out of their criticism is just amusing, or at least that there is nothing wrong with a scene. In order to explain and identify the reasons for what the channels find humorous or leave out, their reactions should be put in contrast with humour theory. There are three main theories of humour that exist. Firstly, the superiority theory, in which humour is claimed to be "an attentive demolition of a person or something connected with a person", as Morreall paraphrases from Roger Scruton (Morreall ch. 2, par. 1). This theory explains most of the negative or non-existent responses and it is relevant to all scenes and their reactions, as demonstrated below. Secondly, the relief theory, to which Freud writes according to Morreall: "In telling or listening to a joke that puts down an individual or group we dislike, similarly, we let out the hostility we usually repress" (Morreall ch. 3, par. 13). It could explain both positive and negative reactions to the third scene and is thus not very important for this paper. The incongruity Theory, finally, describes that we laugh when we encounter something we do not see coming, something unexpected (Morreall ch. 4, par. 1). For this paper, however, it is not very significant.

The first scene gets very different reviews already. CinemaSins, for example, does not actually include Claudette's reaction to Lisa's revelation, they just criticise the fact that the story is untrue (CinemaSins 1:46-1:51). Neither does IHE mention anything more than Lisa's lie (IHE 7:25-7:27). However, criticism comes from FanboyFlicks, who names it "terrible advice" (FanboyFlicks 3:38-3:39) and, even more so, from Channel Awesome, who exclaims: "She just admitted that he hits her and the mother's like 'Johnny doesn't drink'. I know he hits you like a football player's wife but he doesn't drink" (Channel Awesome 11:43-11:53). For CinemaSins and IHE the relief theory cannot be justified because we do not see them laughing. Neither does the incongruity theory make sense because then they would have put the scene in, as they would admit that there is something wrong with it. The superiority theory can be used to explain why two channels did not put the scene in, which is in accordance to the punishment Lisa should receive, as discussed in the section before. Channel Awesome also has a strong reaction towards the second scene, where, upon Johnny's laugh, he says: "that's not funny you sick fuck" (Channel Awesome 15:01-15:05). In contrast to the last scene, IHE is questioning Johnny's laugh (IHE 9:13-9:16) and criticism also comes from FanboyFlicks (FanboyFlicks 17:15-17:25). This means, three of four channels do find something wrong with the story while CinemaSins does not mention it at all. For the latter, the superiority theory would make sense and be in line with the already mentioned punishment of women. Interestingly, CinemaSins do, however, criticise Mark's claim that everything is Lisa's fault by stating that he forgets that they had an affair with each other (CinemaSins 7:18-7:20). Here, the superiority theory would be an explanation as Mark's reaction is not unexpected. Additionally, the relief theory would make sense because of negative feelings towards Mark, which are implied by CinemaSins. None of the other channels actually review this scene which could be explained by the superiority theory. This is in accordance with the points made before on this scene, namely that women are punished in film for being active and embodiments of negative feelings. Additionally, the relief theory might also be true because some channels do not have a high opinion of Lisa.

To put these findings in a wider context, it is important to discuss how Lisa is perceived in general, too, in order to increase the knowledge of the reviewer's values with the help of humour and gender studies. Lisa is viewed quite differently by the channels: both CinemaSins and FanboyFlicks try to be neutral, even though the latter is very criticising about the characters altogether: they mention the bad treatment Johnny receives by all of them and that none of them are very likeable. Channel Awesome seems to have a more positive view towards Lisa while IHE hates her character very much. Although they do say that Mark cannot take himself out of their relationship (IHE 5:29-5:33), they take a very strong negative stance against Lisa.

However, they criticise the treatment towards the female protagonists, exemplified when they talk about a conversation between Lisa and Claudette:

> It's crystal clear that this dialogue was written by a man. A stupid, probably slightly retarded dumbass man, who clearly has no idea what women talk to each other about so he just assumes that all they chat about is men and how they're all pigs but at the same time how important they are to be used for money. (IHE 3:46-4:00)

This all means that in the last scene the superiority theory may be accurate in describing why Channel Awesome did not put the scene in. This is because of their more positive stance towards Lisa which defies the relief theory. For IHE the relief theory can be said to be true because of the opposite feelings while for the others both are possible. In general, the superiority theory is most useful to explain the channels' negative attitudes. This is in line with a quote by Martin that was already mentioned in section one, which says that humour can convey the rules of a community (Martin, *Psychology of Humor* 121) and additionally, "it can be used by individuals to reinforce their own status in a group hierarchy" (Martin, *Psychology of Humor* 120). Martin even gives the example of women being put into an inferior position by men using satire and ridicule (Martin, *Psychology of Humor* 121). Satirical language is often used by the channels, as can be seen in the quote above. Ridicule can not only reinforce stereotypes, it also "places the victim [...] outside the serious world by treating him or her as someone who, quite simply, is not to be taken seriously, something that is mostly done consciously, with a "desire to disparage that person" (Chafe 95). In this particular context, Martin shows that studies found out that people enjoying humour against women often have sexist views (Martin, *Humor and Gender* 127). Platinga writes that the audience develops relationships to the characters (Platinga 380) and these positive and negative feelings function as guidance through the film (Platinga 381). By not criticising the character's actions they are agreeing with them. Mulvey adds that by identifying with a character the person watching is thus in contact with the woman "displayed for his enjoyment" and "gaining control and possession of the woman" (Mulvey 489). It should be added that the personal experience of the audience is important because, as Kuhn stresses, the conscious of the viewer has not been very focused on in recent psychoanalytic film theory (Kuhn 1226). The audience's response, however, is very subjective to a person's own stance toward a particular situation, as Platinga (381) writes, and "[o]ur responses to films depend on our culture's moral order and can function to prescribe and proscribe thought, feeling, behavior and values" (Platinga 389). This means that the negative points of view towards Lisa in general and in the described scenes by some of the channels can be linked directly to what they think is normal and what they would do.

CONCLUSION

In conclusion, Lisa represents the bad and, because of that two of the channels have quite misogynist views towards her, which they show in particular by ignoring scenes where she is mistreated. This stance can be explained by humour, film and gender theory. Lisa is the archetype of the bad woman in the film. She represents pain and fear which can only be fought against by her being punished. In the first scene Lisa lies to her mother, telling her that Johnny hits her. The punishment is ignorance by her mother, representing patriarchal worldviews, for being active when she should be taking everything quietly. The first scene is not mentioned at all by Cinema Sins or IHE, which can be theorised through the superiority theory, which states that someone is laughing because they are feeling above someone. The channels may already feel very connected to Johnny as a screen surrogate. The second scene is the story of a woman who got hit by a lover she cheated on. This is criticised by all but one channel. CinemaSins, not mentioning this part of the scene, may do that because of a desire to keep the rules as they are, which is in accordance to the superiority theory. In general, this scene punishes not just Lisa but all women, represented by the unknown female of the story. In the third scene, Lisa is made responsible for Johnny's death by Mark because she has an affair with him and he does not feel responsible. She is punished for being active and seducing Mark, thus taking his and the viewer's power away. Only CinemaSins is reviewing this scene, saying that Mark, too, is at fault for the affair. Humour, in general, can enforce stereotypes and especially satirical content can be used against someone. Because people laughing at sexist jokes are often sexist themselves, what the channels put and do not put into their reviews says much about their stance towards women. Misogynistic worldviews can be shown in what they find funny but not wrong, and thus do not put in a video, in contrast to what they do put in because they think it is bad. CinemaSins is providing the most sexist worldview, because they ignore two scenes at least two of the other channels find something wrong with. IHE does not mention the first or the third scene, also suggesting a misogynistic worldview. FanboyFlicks and Channel Awesome seem to be the least sexist, only leaving out the third scene, where Mark's reaction could be put on him not thinking clearly, as mentioned at the beginning. The sexist values that are displayed by at least two of the channels by their ignorance towards problematic scenes in the film are worrying and the way that the traditional film works to enforce these stereotypes makes that worse.

REFERENCES

Chafe, Wallace. *The Importance of Not Being Earnest: The Feeling behind Laughter and Humor.* Amsterdam: John Benjamins, 2007.

Eco, Umberto. "Casablanca: Cult Movies and Intertextual Collage". *Faith in Fakes: Essays*, trans. William Weaver. London: Secker and Warburg, 1986. 197–200.

Kuhn, Annette. "The state of film and media feminism". *Journal of Women in Culture and Society* 30 (2004). 1222-1228.

Martin, Rod A. "Humor & Gender: An Overview of Psychological Research". *Gender and Humor. Interdisciplinary and International Perspectives.* ed. Delia Chiaro & Raffaella Baccolini. Oxford: Routledge, 2014. 123-146.

Martin, Rod A. *The Psychology of Humor: An Integrative Approach.* Amsterdam: Elsevier, 2007.

Morreall, John. *Philosophy of Humor.* 28. 09. 2016. Stanford Encyclopedia of Philosophy. 01. 08. 2017 <https://plato.stanford.edu/entries/humor/#Rel>.

Mulvey, Laura. "Visual Pleasure and Narrative Cinema". *Film & Theory. An Anthology.* ed. Robert Stam & Toby Miller. Massachusets: Blackwell, 2000. 483-494.

Platinga, Carl. "Notes on Spectator Emotion and Ideological Film Criticism". *Film Theory & Philosophy.* ed. Richard Allen & Murray Smith. Oxford: Clarendon Press, 1997. 372-393.

Williams, Linda. "Film Bodies: Gender, Genre and Excess". *Film & Theory. An Anthology.* ed. Robert Stam & Toby Miller. Massachusets: Blackwell, 2000. 207-221.

The Room. Written by Tommy Wiseau. Directed by Tommy Wiseau. YouTube. 2003. (https://www.youtube.com/watch?v=C6D9Oifh9zU) 13. 8. 2017.

The Room - The Search For The Worst – IHE. I Hate Everything. YouTube. 21. 11. 2014. (https://www.youtube.com/watch?v=k-T4p6XFCUc) 13. 8. 2017.

Everything Wrong With The Room In 8 Minutes Or Less. CinemaSins. YouTube. 29. 01. 2013. (https://www.youtube.com/watch?v=mvuwldnG7c0) 13. 08. 2017.

The Room – BAD MOVIES. FanboyFlicks. YouTube. 14. 02. 2014. (https://www.youtube.com/watch?v=JwGvPWRcnQk) 13. 08. 2017.

The Room – Nostalgia Critic. Channel Awesome. YouTube. 25. 04. 2015. (https://www.youtube.com/watch?v=Tri9i3WtXLc) 13. 08. 2017.

YOUR KNOWLEDGE HAS VALUE

- We will publish your bachelor's and master's thesis, essays and papers

- Your own eBook and book - sold worldwide in all relevant shops

- Earn money with each sale

Upload your text at www.GRIN.com
and publish for free